W 12/14 W 2/18 W 3/22

MR - - '73

THE ANCIENT WORLD

ANCIENT MESOPOTAMIA

BY ALLISON LASSIEUR

CHILDREN'S PRESS®
AN IMPRINT OF SCHOLASTIC INC.
NEW YORK TORONTO LONDON AUCKLAND SYDNEY
MEXICO CITY NEW DELHI HONG KONG
DANBURY, CONNECTICUT

Content Consultant
Kevin M. McGeough, PhD
Associate Professor
Department of Geography (Archaeology)
University of Lethbridge
Lethbridge, Alberta, Canada

Library of Congress Cataloging-in-Publication Data
Lassieur, Allison.
  Ancient Mesopotamia/by Allison Lassieur.
    p. cm.—(The ancient world)
  Includes bibliographical references and index.
  ISBN: 978-0-531-25182-9 (lib. bdg.)   ISBN: 978-0-531-25982-5 (pbk.)
  1. Iraq—Civilization—To 634—Juvenile literature. I. Title.
  DS69.5.L36 2012
  935—dc23   2012002436

JOURNEY BACK TO ANCIENT MESOPOTAMIA

People first settled between the Tigris and Euphrates Rivers in about 10,000 BCE.

The Code of Hammurabi is the oldest known example of written laws.

The ancient Mesopotamians created written documents by etching symbols into soft clay tablets.

TABLE OF CONTENTS

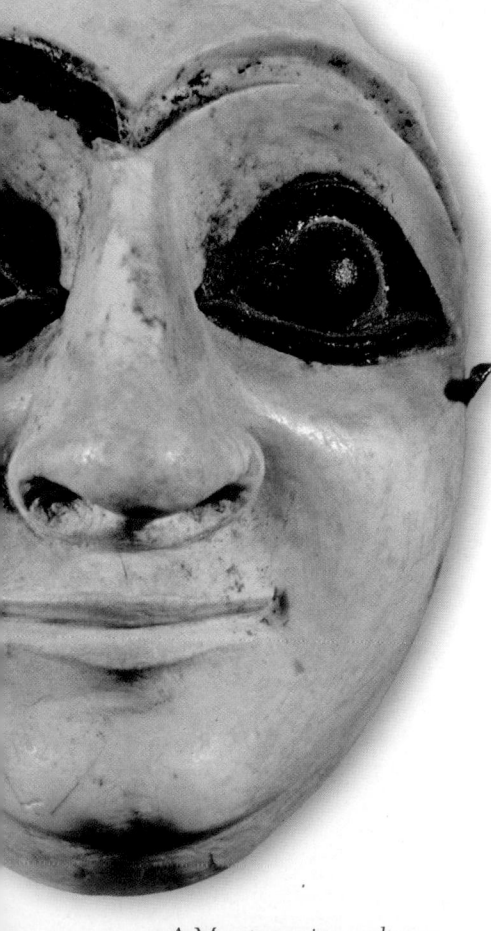

A Mesopotamian sculpture dating back to the twenty-seventh century BCE

A carving from the Code of Hammurabi

CONQUERING BABYLON

In 539 BCE, Mesopotamia was one of the richest kingdoms in the world. King Cyrus of Persia wanted to claim it as his own. Mesopotamia's capital city, Babylon, was the jewel in the crown.

King Cyrus of Persia ruled over a vast area during the sixth century BCE.

It was the largest, most advanced city in Mesopotamia. Cyrus knew that if he controlled Babylon, he would control the world.

The ancient Greek historian Herodotus recorded the way Cyrus accomplished his goal. According to this record, Cyrus gathered his Persian armies and set out for Babylon. When he arrived, he found that a large Babylonian force had camped outside the city walls. The Persians and the Babylonians fought fiercely. Cyrus was victorious, but the Babylonian army fled into the walled city and slammed the gates behind them before he could get inside.

The Persians could not attack the city because the mighty Euphrates River, which flowed into the city, stood in their way. Eventually, Cyrus came up with a plan. Instead of crossing the Euphrates River, he would move it. The Persian soldiers set to work digging in a marshy area near the river. They created a large basin into which the river could flow. Cyrus's plan worked, and the Euphrates River flowed

Herodotus's writings are the main source of our knowledge of King Cyrus.

Babylon stood along both sides of the Euphrates River.

into the new basin. Now Cyrus and his army waited for the perfect time to attack. They found their opportunity during a huge celebration in Babylon. It was no trouble for the Persians to march over the newly shallow riverbed and sweep into Babylon before anyone knew what was going on. The army was able to seize Babylon without any bloodshed. Cyrus claimed the city and became king of Babylon. He eventually became known as Cyrus the Great, one of Mesopotamia's greatest rulers.

This eighteenth century illustration depicts Cyrus and his men entering Babylon.

Cyrus ruled over Babylon until his death around 529 BCE.

empire (EM-pire) a group of countries or states that have the same ruler

archaeologists (ahr-kee-AH-luh-jists) people who study the past, which often involves digging up old buildings, objects, and bones and examining them carefully

Today, Herodotus's account of Cyrus's conquest of Babylon is considered more fiction than fact. However, it remains a gripping action-adventure story. Just like in many other great stories, the hero won the prize. But by the time Cyrus took Babylon and absorbed it into his enormous Persian **Empire**, the city had already begun to fall. His victory in Babylon signaled the end of the great empires of Mesopotamia.

Babylon lived on as a part of the Persian Empire for the next several hundred years. It was the center of culture, but not of strength. A series of conquerors captured it from one another. By 275 CE, the city was almost totally empty. It would be hundreds of years before **archaeologists** in the nineteenth century began excavating the city and rediscovering its splendors.

Babylon was the final city and culture considered to be Mesopotamian, but it was far from the only one. Most people believe that Mesopotamia was one large civilization that existed for many centuries, but that was not the case. Ancient Mesopotamia was a land of many cultures. The earliest civilization of Sumer, the mighty Assyrians, and the rich Babylonians were only a few of the groups that existed during the long history of Mesopotamia. The story of Mesopotamia is the history of these groups, which rose, fought, ruled, and fell alongside one another over the course of thousands of years.

Reconstructed ruins of Babylon stand in what is now Iraq.

CHAPTER ONE

THE WORLD'S FIRST CIVILIZATION

Ancient Mesopotamia was one of the world's first great civilizations. Its people were responsible for early innovations in writing, **agriculture**, city building, and the

The ancient Mesopotamians were responsible for many important innovations in agriculture and architecture.

recording of history. Tens of thousands of people lived in its enormous, beautiful cities.

Throughout Mesopotamian history, politics changed and many different rulers rose to power and eventually fell. Cultures grew, became powerful, and were overthrown by stronger cultures that moved in to take their places. None of this happened in a simple, straight succession, however. At times, Mesopotamia was controlled by several different groups at once, with each group claiming a specific region. A long line of kings and cultures attacked and overtook the city of Babylon, only for each culture to be overthrown by a later rival. Despite the various origins of these people, however, they all considered themselves to be Mesopotamian.

Babylon went through many changes in leadership throughout its history.

agriculture (AG-ri-kuhl-chur) the raising of crops and animals

fertile (FUR-tuhl)
good for growing crops
and plants

nomads (NO-madz)
members of a
community who travel
from place to place
instead of living in the
same place all the time

*Mesopotamia's earliest
people hunted, fished,
and collected food from
wild plants.*

Before the Beginning: The First Farmers

Around 10,000 BCE, the first humans settled in a vast, **fertile** region between the Tigris and Euphrates Rivers in West Asia, in parts of what are now Iraq, Syria, and Turkey. No one knows exactly who these people were, when they arrived, or where they came from. They were **nomads**, groups of people who traveled from place to place. They were also hunter-gatherers, which means they hunted game and gathered wild foods instead of growing crops.

At some point, these people realized they could grow their food themselves but that they needed to stay in one place to do it.

The Past Is Present
SETTLING DOWN

The shift from nomadic life to farming is one of the most dramatic events in human history. This change happened independently in many parts of the world, including ancient Egypt and ancient India, at around the same time. However, it was especially prominent in northern Mesopotamia, where there was enough rainfall to support raising crops and animals.

Today, almost all of the world's people live in permanent homes, whether in huge cities or small rural settlements. However, some peoples continue to practice the nomadic lifestyles of their ancestors. Some modern nomads travel almost constantly, searching for animals to hunt and food to gather. Others, called pastoral nomads, move from place to place with herds of livestock. They search for areas where their animals can graze and often stay in the same location for longer periods of time. Some people are only partially nomadic. They stay in the same place long enough to grow crops but do not create permanent settlements.

*Later settlers learned
that they could plant
seeds to grow their own
food crops.*

The process of settling down and learning to grow food took thousands of years. At first, the people combined simple gardening with hunting and gathering. Later they began to grow crops on a larger scale. They also began to **domesticate** animals such as sheep and goats for milk, meat, and wool.

Between 7000 and 4000 BCE, three main groups lived in Mesopotamia: the Hassuna, Samarra, and Halaf cultures. Little is known about these people except that they made beautiful pottery, used stone tools, developed early plows, and figured out how to spin thread from **flax** and wool.

The Ubaid period of Mesopotamia lasted from about 6200 to 4000 BCE. The Ubaid culture started out as farmers but gradually began to settle in large groups, creating the first villages. Archaeologists first discovered Ubaid artifacts in the village of Tell al-Ubaid. They have since found several other Ubaid villages throughout Mesopotamia. The Ubaid culture was a sophisticated group of people who made knives, hoes, bricks, sculpture, and painted pottery. They also built temples, showing that they had an organized religion. They created **irrigation** systems by digging ditches from the nearby rivers into their fields, where they grew wheat and barley.

Archaeologists have uncovered a variety of artifacts left behind by the ancient Halaf people.

domesticate (duh-MES-ti-kate) to tame plants or animals so they can be used by humans

flax (FLAKS) a plant with blue flowers that produces oil and fiber

irrigation (ir-uh-GAY-shuhn) the use of artificial means, such as channels and pipes, to supply water to crops

Archaeologists extensively excavated the former site of Eridu during the late 1940s.

THE RISE OF THE SUMERIAN CIVILIZATION

Sometime around 4000 BCE, a new group of people emerged in Mesopotamia. These people, the Sumerians, were unlike earlier Mesopotamians. They figured out how to build elaborate irrigation systems and canals, which allowed them to grow more crops. These crops could support larger villages, so the Sumerians built cities that became cultural and religious centers. Eventually, they began to spread throughout larger areas.

SUMERIAN CITY-STATES

Sumer wasn't a single country or kingdom, but a collection of city-states. A city-state consisted of one powerful city and several smaller cities and villages that worked together like an independent state. Many city-states began as small villages near large areas of irrigated farmland. Archaeologists have discovered many Sumerian cities that were the capitals of larger city-states. Some of the best known include Ur, Kish, Lagash, and Eridu. These cities were huge urban areas with thousands of people. Fields of grain and pastures filled with animals surrounded the cities and provided food for the people. Thousands of farmers, herdsmen, and fishermen lived in the outlying areas. At the center of each city rose a fine temple dedicated to the city's patron god.

Eridu was formed around seven thousand years ago along the banks of the Euphrates River. The ancient Sumerians considered it to be the first city, the city of kings. Eridu was a religious center dedicated to the water god Enki. At that time, the land around Eridu was filled with marshland waters from the Euphrates. Its location was especially sacred.

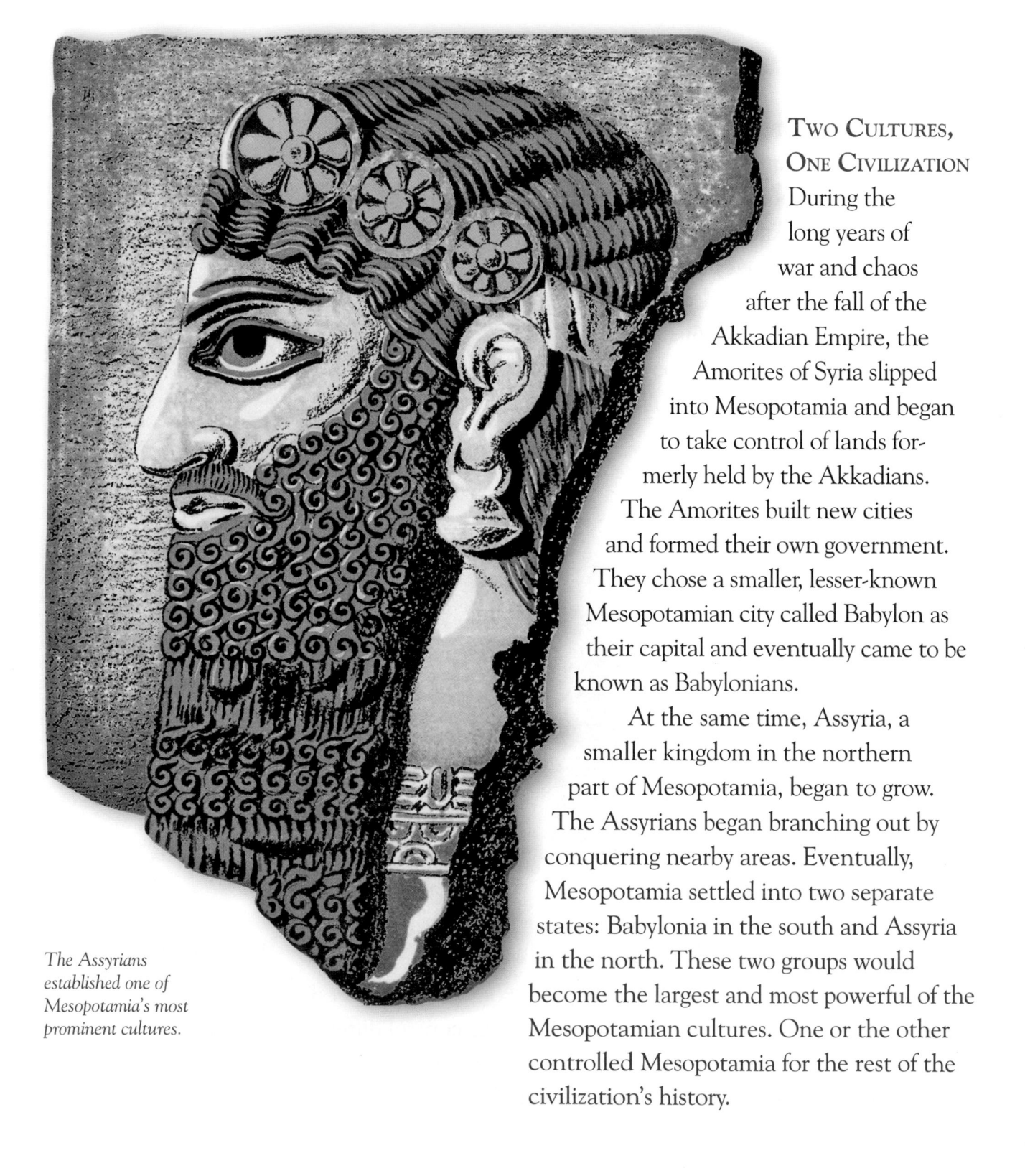

The Assyrians established one of Mesopotamia's most prominent cultures.

TWO CULTURES, ONE CIVILIZATION

During the long years of war and chaos after the fall of the Akkadian Empire, the Amorites of Syria slipped into Mesopotamia and began to take control of lands formerly held by the Akkadians. The Amorites built new cities and formed their own government. They chose a smaller, lesser-known Mesopotamian city called Babylon as their capital and eventually came to be known as Babylonians.

At the same time, Assyria, a smaller kingdom in the northern part of Mesopotamia, began to grow. The Assyrians began branching out by conquering nearby areas. Eventually, Mesopotamia settled into two separate states: Babylonia in the south and Assyria in the north. These two groups would become the largest and most powerful of the Mesopotamian cultures. One or the other controlled Mesopotamia for the rest of the civilization's history.

KING HAMMURABI AND THE OLD BABYLONIAN PERIOD

In about 1792 BCE, Hammurabi became the sixth king of Babylon. By then, Babylonia had grown to include many smaller cities and villages. Most historians consider Hammurabi to be the founder of the Old Babylonian Empire.

Hammurabi extended his kingdom even farther by conquering city-states such as Uruk and Isin. Back in the capital city of Babylon, he ordered dozens of large-scale projects, such as new irrigation systems, agricultural improvements, and the construction of new temples and buildings. It was under his rule that Babylonia became one of the most prosperous and powerful kingdoms in Mesopotamia.

After his death around 1750 BCE, the kingdom of Old Babylonia crumbled under the rule of a series of weak kings. However, Babylon had such a strong reputation as a center of culture and learning that it continued to be a powerful and respected city.

Hammurabi is one of the most well known of Babylon's many rulers.

Hammurabi's strong leadership helped Babylon to grow rapidly during his reign.

NEW ENEMIES, NEW IDEAS

As the Old Babylonian rulers grew weaker, the culture of another people, the Hittites, was growing stronger. The Hittites originally came from Anatolia, in what is now Turkey. They began to invade Mesopotamia in about 1600 BCE. In 1595 BCE, they attacked and overthrew Babylon, but decided not to settle there. Instead, the Hittites remained farther north and west. The Hittite Empire ruled Anatolia, Syria, and upper Mesopotamia for about three hundred years, until around 1200 BCE.

The Hittites conquered Babylon, but did not take it over as their own.

plundered (PLUHN-durd) stole things by force

At the same time the Hittites controlled northern Mesopotamia, another group, the Kassites, gained power. The Kassites attacked Babylon and took it from the Hittites in about 1570 BCE and then ruled lower Mesopotamia until around 1158 BCE. During their rule, the Kassites fully adopted many of the customs and religious beliefs of the Babylonians.

ASSYRIA AND THE CONQUEST OF MESOPOTAMIA

A new enemy appeared in 1234 BCE, when an Assyrian king named Tukulti-Ninurta attacked Babylon. He **plundered** the grand city and proclaimed himself king of Babylon, Sumer, Akkad, and Assyria. His victory began the Assyrian control of Mesopotamia. The Assyrians maintained power for about two hundred years, overthrowing many outlying groups. The Assyrian king Sennacherib ruled from 704 to 681 BCE. He moved the capital of Assyria to the ancient city of Nineveh. Nineveh became the symbol of power and wealth in the Assyrian kingdom.

Ashurbanipal was the last great Assyrian king, ruling from 668 to 627 BCE. Assyria remained a powerful kingdom under his command. Soon after his reign, however, Assyria's strength began to diminish. In 612 BCE, many conquered cities, including Babylon, rebelled against their Assyrian overlords. At that point, Assyria seems to disappear from history. Scholars suspect that its cities were raided and destroyed. Many of its citizens were sold as slaves to other cultures.

THE RISE AND FALL OF THE NEO-BABYLONIAN EMPIRE

The Babylonian ruler Nabopolassar captured the Assyrian city of Nineveh in 612 BCE and established the Neo-Babylonian empire.

This stone altar depicts Tukulti-Ninurta in prayer.

His son, Nebuchadnezzar II, brought Neo-Babylonia its greatest fame. Under his rule, Babylon was rebuilt into a huge, dazzling city filled with new temples and palace buildings, gates, walls, and paved roads. Babylon's beauty, color, and luxury became legendary. It was the largest city known at the time, covering more than 2,500 acres (1,012 hectares). One of its features, the Hanging Gardens, was one of the Seven Wonders of the Ancient World.

During his reign, Nebuchadnezzar II built Babylon into the largest city of its time.

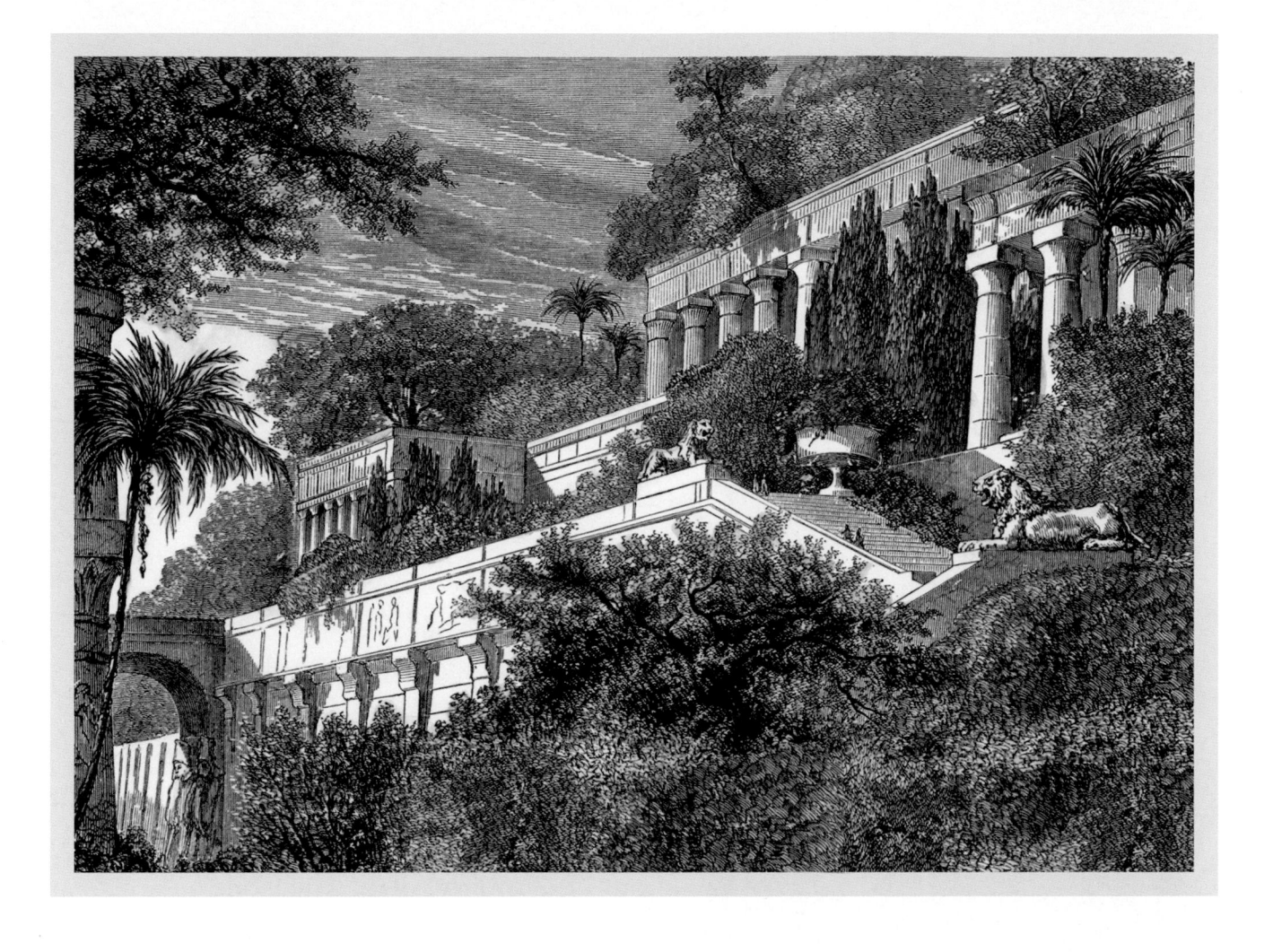

But the glory of Babylon was not to last for long. After Nebuchadnezzar's death around 561 BCE, weak and ineffectual kings once again controlled Babylonia. Economic problems, famine, sickness, and political fighting weakened the civilization further. Outside Mesopotamia, a culture known as the Persians was growing in strength.

In 539 BCE, the Persian leader Cyrus led his army into Babylon and captured the city. Cyrus installed a Persian governor to control Babylon. The Babylonians rebelled against the Persian control, but they never regained their city or their culture.

The Hanging Gardens of Babylon are legendary for their incredible beauty.

CHAPTER TWO
KINGS, GODS, AND LAWGIVERS

In 1901, a group of archaeologists were excavating the ancient Iranian city of Susa when they discovered a remarkable object: a 7-foot-tall (2.13 meter), black stone monument inscribed in the ancient Akkadian language. It was the Code of Hammurabi, the earliest written laws. Hammurabi was an Amorite king who ruled from 1792 to 1750 BCE. The Code of Hammurabi was a set of laws inscribed in an attempt to show the people of Mesopotamia that Hammurabi was a just ruler. The code covered everything from how much to pay a veterinarian for treating farm animals to how

The top of the Code of Hammurabi displays an illustration of Hammurabi himself.

Words and pictures alike help to illustrate the laws proclaimed by the Code of Hammurabi.

various crimes should be punished. However, comparisons to legal records from the time, such as court cases and legal contracts, show that the code did not always match up with actual legal practices.

Mesopotamian government was influenced by geography, religion, and the culture of the people who were in power. The downfall of one culture didn't always mean the downfall of its system of government. New rulers often adopted the government systems of the people they conquered or combined them with their own traditions to create something new.

The different governments and cultures of ancient Mesopotamia were in almost constant warfare throughout the civilization's history. They fought to protect themselves, thinking that if they conquered more lands they would eliminate threats to their power. When they wanted wealth, they took it by force and then taxed the people they conquered, took their lands and resources, and forced people into slavery. They also fought for their gods, who were believed to grant kings the responsibility to conquer more land and bring more worshippers to the temples. The different governments that came into being were shaped by all of these forces.

Mesopotamian kings fought to take new lands and accumulate more wealth.

THE LAWS OF THE LAND

The Code of Hammurabi helps to explain how ancient Mesopotamian government was run. It describes specific crimes and punishments, some of which might seem harsh today. For example, it declares that a son who hits his father should have both of his hands cut off. It also states that a man who puts out the eye of another man should have one of his own eyes put out. The code outlined the laws regarding such everyday topics as marriage, divorce, and taxes as well.

While some of the punishments described in the code are more extreme than those of most modern legal systems, much

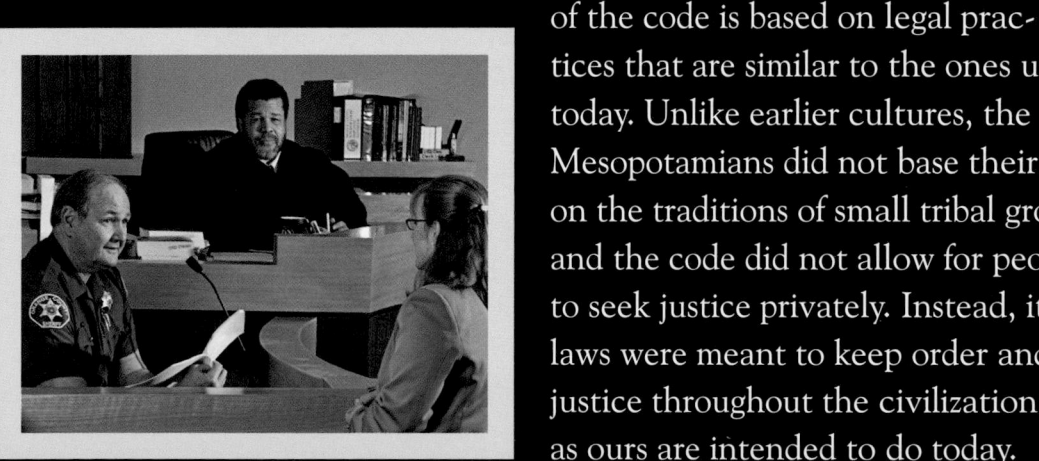

of the code is based on legal practices that are similar to the ones used today. Unlike earlier cultures, the Mesopotamians did not base their laws on the traditions of small tribal groups, and the code did not allow for people to seek justice privately. Instead, its laws were meant to keep order and justice throughout the civilization, just as ours are intended to do today.

Kings often consulted with priests and other advisers.

INVENTING GOVERNMENT

Mesopotamia had one of the first legal systems, with laws decreed by the king. People involved in disputes often took their cases to government officials or the king himself, who pronounced judgment. The people involved in the dispute had to swear by the gods that they would abide by the king's decisions.

One of the most important government jobs was that of the scribe. Scribes kept records of taxes, the amount of farmland in different regions, the price of slaves, and the amount of trade goods coming into and out of the city.

Laws were proclaimed by the king and carried out by lesser government officials.

The Kings of Ancient Sumer

No one knows how or when the Sumerians developed their earliest government systems, but by around 3000 BCE they had created large city-states, each with its own ruler. The Sumerians believed that their kings were chosen by each city's patron god. The king looked out for his people, providing security and safety as a god would. In some early Sumerian cities, the ruler was given the title of *en*, which means "lord." Later rulers were known as *lugal*, or "king," or *ensi*, meaning "governor." It's not clear exactly what these titles signified, and it's likely that one person could use several titles at once. An assembly of advisers assisted each king.

Sumerian kings were responsible for the military. They led armies into war and made treaties with neighboring lands. Friendly relations with neighbors helped to expand a city-state's trade, which brought wealth. Kings were also expected to build and care for the city's temples and to organize official religious ceremonies. The kings and their wives, known as *nins*, were often seen as divine couples. They lived in the temples, which were centers of both religion and government.

Eventually, the rulers of the early Sumerian city-states began to separate themselves from their roles in religious life. Slowly, leadership split in two. The king controlled the government and military, and the priests controlled the temples. The king was still considered the supreme ruler and a representative of the god, but he was able to concentrate more on running the government and less on managing the city-state's religious life.

The King Lists

"After the kingship descended from heaven, the kingship was in Eridu. In Eridu, Alulim became king; he ruled for 28800 years."

Sumerian kings were believed to have a very close relationship with their cities' patron gods.

Kings and their wives enjoyed the finest foods and comforts available.

So begins the ancient Sumerian King List, an ancient stone tablet that lists all the Sumerian rulers, where they lived, and the years they were in power. Several other ancient king lists have also been found, providing some understanding of how the city-states interacted with one another. The lists record when each dynasty fell and which new ruler replaced it. They also indicate where the seat of power moved after each upheaval. Most king lists are in fragments, but combining all the information from the various stone tablets gives a complete list. The Sumerian King List is the oldest and includes the names of the first Mesopotamian kings.

KINGS AS GODS

Sargon of Akkad conquered Mesopotamia around 2350 BCE, and his descendants continued to rule for several generations. The fourth Akkadian king, Naram-Sin, declared that he was not simply a representative of the god, but a divine being himself. This concept of divine kings continued through the end of the Akkadian period, but afterward was mostly abandoned, though later Mesopotamian rulers were still thought to be chosen directly by the gods. The

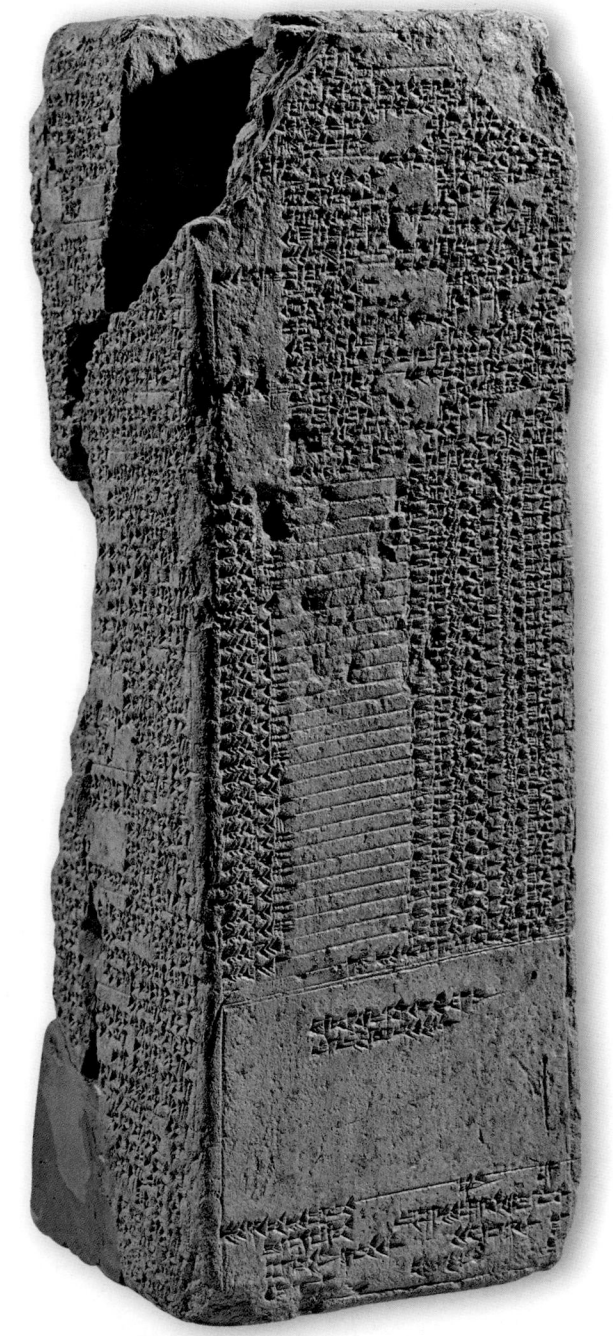

The Sumerian King List has been an invaluable resource in understanding the history of ancient Mesopotamia.

kingship was **hereditary**, but on occasion a king was defeated, and the conqueror took his place as the divine ruler.

After gaining control of Babylonia, the Kassites added another layer to Mesopotamian government by dividing the kingdom into principalities, or sections, that were ruled by king-appointed governors. They also created a class of warrior-nobles that wasn't divine but had power in the different provinces.

When the Assyrians ruled Mesopotamia, they continued the idea of an absolute ruler who was also the high priest of Ashur, the main god of Assyria. As kings conquered new lands, they put provincial governors in charge. These governors kept a tight grip on the conquered local people.

Mesopotamian government remained similar under Babylonian control, with one central king holding power granted by the gods. Babylonian rule was much more peaceful than Assyrian rule, especially under the control of King Nebuchadnezzar. His provincial governors still ruled their areas, but the focus was on prosperity and peace rather than conquest and control.

RUNNING THE GOVERNMENT

Each Mesopotamian king had officials who were in charge of the day-to-day running of the government. The priests, including the high priest of the main god, were at the top of the organization. Lesser priests oversaw the running of the temples and local religious ceremonies. Armies were led by commanders who were usually chosen by the king. Commanders were in charge of organizing and training the troops. There was usually an official who was in charge of maintaining good relations with friendly neighboring kingdoms and who welcomed foreign **ambassadors** into

Ashur was considered to be the national god of Assyria.

A variety of government officials helped the king rule.

court. Below these royal officials was an army of servants, cupbearers, cooks, slaves, nurses for the royal children, maids for the royal wives, scribes, and sometimes royal artists and sculptors.

Each large town or city had a council of elders tasked with hearing disputes and making judgments. People brought complaints of crimes to the council, who heard their arguments, examined any evidence, and took witness testimonies. Anyone who testified had to swear an oath on a sacred symbol of the local god. Most people eagerly took the oath, because telling a lie meant being cursed by the gods. If the council could not reach a decision, it often held a "trial by river." The accused would be thrown in a river. If he swam to shore, he was judged to be innocent. If he drowned, he was considered to have been taken by the river god. This meant he was guilty. Once the verdict was given, it was written on a clay tablet and filed away.

Prisoners and criminals were treated harshly in ancient Mesopotamia.

To Become King and God

A Mesopotamian king had to make sure that his throne would be in good hands when he died, so at some point during his reign he would choose an heir. The heir was usually one of the king's sons. After the king made his decision, the priests consulted the gods and

Each king chose an heir whom he believed would continue his legacy.

44

A variety of upper-class citizens were present when new heirs were presented.

gave their blessing to the heir. After that, the king called an assembly of nobles, government officials, visiting dignitaries from other kingdoms, and sometimes ordinary citizens to officially present the new heir. The people swore to accept him, and amid cheers and shouts, the heir would ceremoniously enter the *bit-riduti*, a special house reserved for the heir to the throne. The heir would also be presented to the army, which swore loyalty to him as well. Once the heir was made official, he could command military expeditions and begin helping the king with government duties.

The Substitute King

It was vital that the king be kept safe if he was ever in danger, so the Mesopotamians created the job of substitute king. If **omens** predicted the king's death, the real king went into hiding and a temporary substitute king was chosen. This person was usually a prisoner of war, a criminal condemned to death, a political enemy, or a slave. The substitute king would be dressed in the royal robes, given a pretend queen, and be allowed to live in the royal palace. He was given all the luxuries of the real king, including huge feasts, comfortable beds, jewels, and musicians. But there was a catch. When the danger to the king had passed, the substitute could not go free. He had to "go to his fate," which in Mesopotamia was an expression that meant death.

Substitute kings enjoyed, for a short time, all the privileges of the real king.

CHAPTER THREE

LAND OF EDEN

Mesopotamia was not the name that the Mesopotamian people themselves gave their land. Rather, it was Greek historians and travelers who called the area Mesopotamia,

Mesopotamian society thrived largely due to its location along the Tigris and Euphrates Rivers.

from the Greek *mesos* (middle) and *potamos* (river). The Mesopotamian people knew their lands by the names of the various independent cities and kingdoms they lived in. Today, Mesopotamia lies in what are now Iraq and parts of Syria and Turkey.

The Tigris and Euphrates Rivers defined life in Mesopotamia. Most of Mesopotamia was located in the lowlands of the basins of these two rivers. This region contains some of the most fertile lands in the world. The Tigris and Euphrates Rivers stretch about 1,200 miles (1,931 kilometers) and 1,700 miles (2,736 km), respectively, from their headwaters in eastern Turkey all the way to the Persian Gulf.

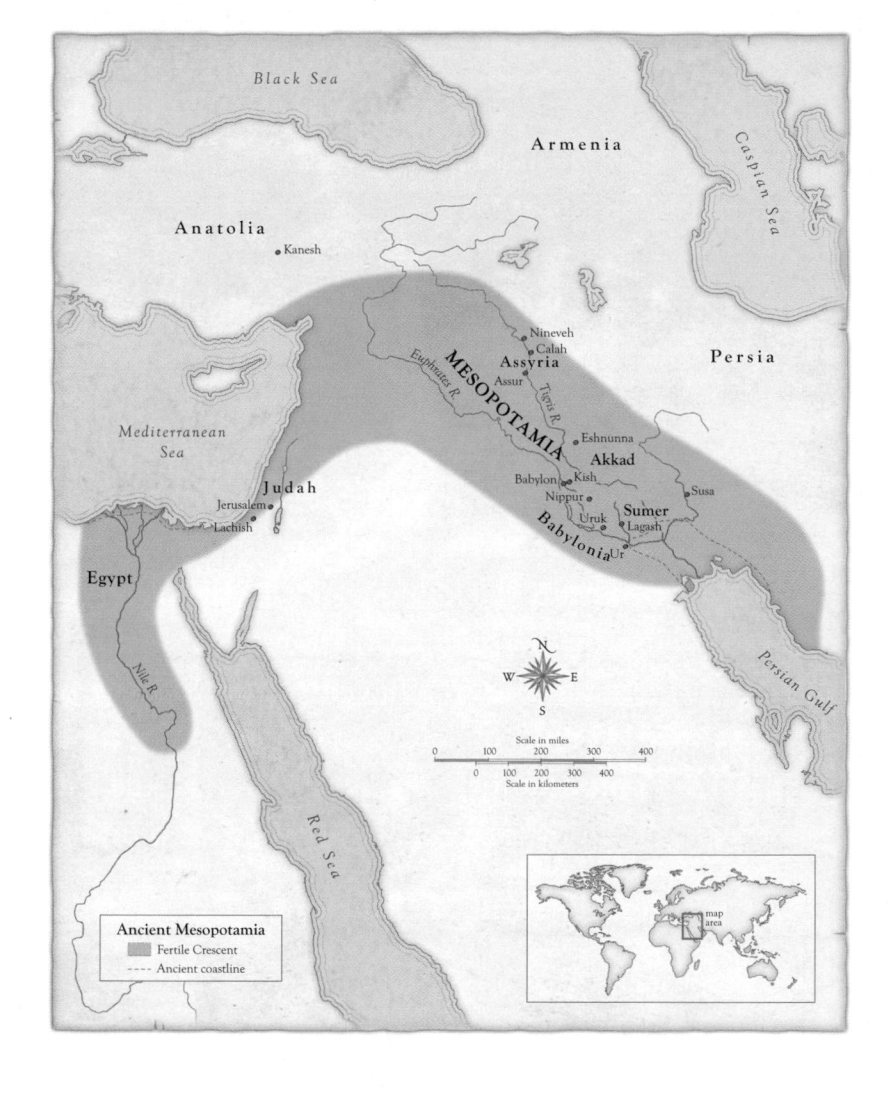

Today, the Tigris and Euphrates merge into the Shatt Al-Arab River before they empty into the Persian Gulf, but in ancient Mesopotamian times they flowed separately into the gulf. At that time, the gulf extended almost 150 miles (241 km) farther inland than it does today. Cities that are now buried beneath desert sands, such as Ur and Eridu, were once located along the coast of the sea.

The Past Is Present

PARADISE LOST?

The Fertile Crescent, where Mesopotamia was founded, was once home to some of the greatest farmland in the world, but it is now drying up. For the last several years, the governments of Turkey and Syria have built dams on the Tigris and Euphrates Rivers, blocking the water from flowing to the farmlands. Droughts have ravaged the area as well. The land, which had been black and fertile for thousands of years, is cracked and dry. Farmers are abandoning their homes, and efforts to bring more water to the area have stopped. In some places, the rivers have dried up completely. In others, only a trickle of water remains. Some scientists predict that the Fertile Crescent will become a desert by the end of the twenty-first century.

THE FERTILE CRESCENT AND THE DAWN OF AGRICULTURE

Mesopotamia is part of a much larger area known as the
Fertile Crescent, which begins along the eastern shore of the
Mediterranean Sea and curves around to the Persian Gulf. The
Fertile Crescent was among the richest farming areas in the world.
Today, it is often called the cradle of civilization. In the northern

The Shatt Al-Arab River connects towns and cities along the Tigris and Euphrates until it empties into the Persian Gulf.

areas, early farmers could rely on good rainfall for their crops. In the south, the rivers deposited dark silt on the land during yearly floods. In both the northern and southern areas of the Fertile Crescent, ancient farmers cultivated this rich soil and fed thousands of people. Today, countries such as Iraq and Iran still rely on the lands of the Fertile Crescent for some of their food.

The richness of this soil, along with the help of new irrigation systems, transformed Mesopotamia from a land of nomads into one of history's greatest civilizations. The region's people could

The Persian Gulf helps form one side of the Fertile Crescent.

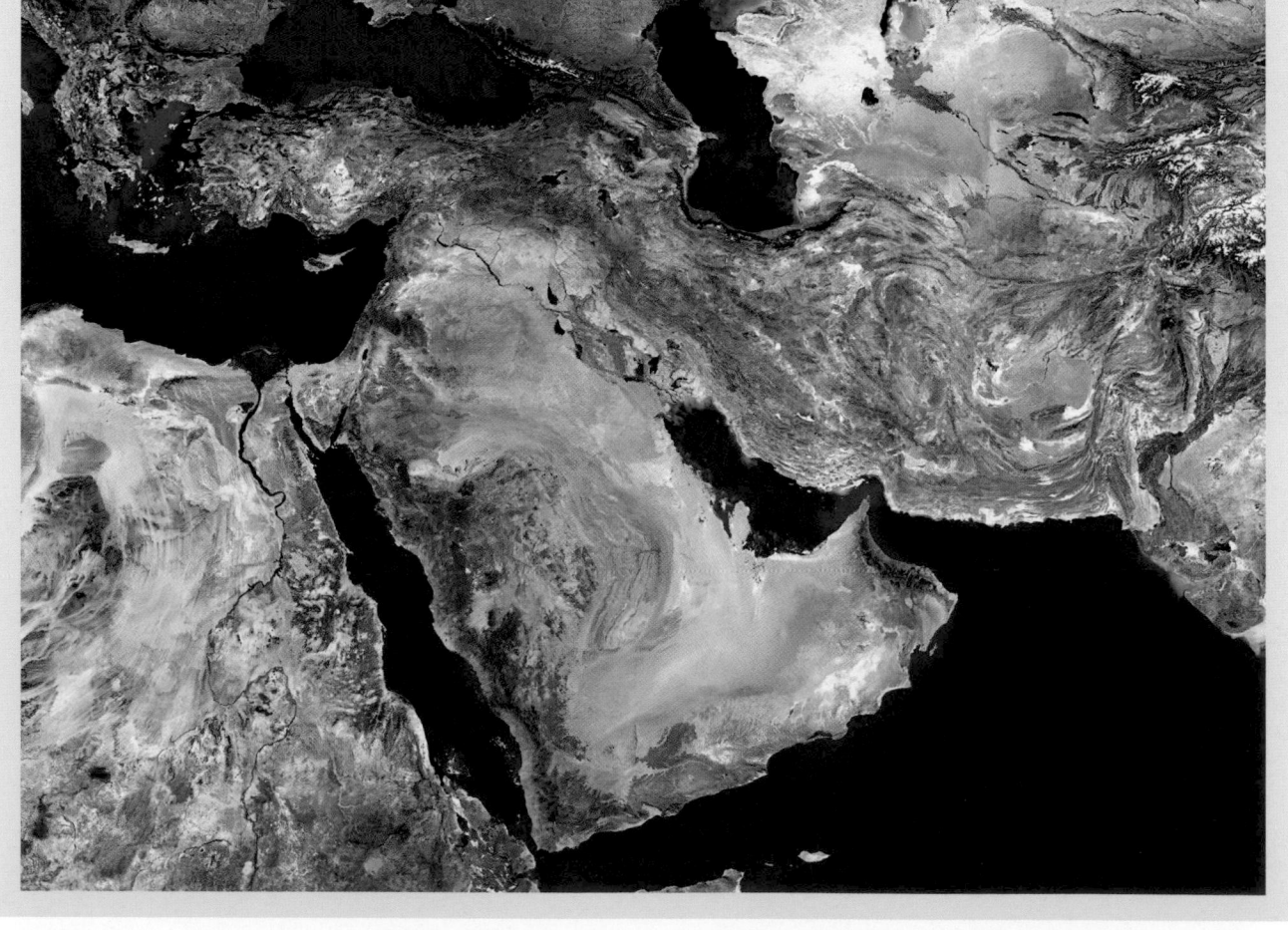

Mesopotamia began to grow rapidly as more people turned to farming as their main source of food.

grow much more food than they needed for themselves. Some people began spending their time on things other than farming, such as making pottery or weaving cloth. Farmers began to build permanent homes near their fields. Slowly, these small groups of people grew larger. They were the beginning of the earliest cultures of Mesopotamia.

To gather building materials, workers loaded heavy stones into containers and carried them out of quarries on foot.

GEOGRAPHY = LIFE

Mesopotamia is made up of different regions, each with its own geography. The land, climate, and resources affected the ways people lived. Surrounding the Mesopotamian river valleys are deserts, mountains, and the sea. The Syrian Desert is west, the Persian Gulf is south, and the mountains of Turkey and Iran rise to the north and east. The rivers begin in the Taurus Mountains and flow southeast through the flat, **alluvial** plain and on to the sea.

Southern Mesopotamia is made up of marshy areas and wide, flat, barren plains, cut by rivers that snake through the landscape. Mesopotamians learned to irrigate the land along the banks of the rivers to bring water to their crops. Spring floods brought life-giving water, but also danger that could damage cities and farmlands. The rich lands were so fertile, however, that it was worth the risk.

Northern Mesopotamia is made up of hills and plains, and the rivers flowed through rocky areas that made the waters more permanent and predictable. The land there wasn't as rich as in the south, but the climate and croplands were good for raising livestock such as cattle, donkeys, and goats. Early Mesopotamians also used timber, metals, and stone from the mountains nearby.

MESOPOTAMIAN BLACK GOLD

The ancient Mesopotamians grew a huge variety of foods, including wheat, rye, barley, sesame, fruits, vegetables, and herbs. In addition to life-giving water, the rivers provided clay, which the Mesopotamians used to make bricks and writing tablets. The area around the rivers provided bitumen, a natural asphalt-like substance. Bitumen seeped out of the ground from beds, especially near the Euphrates. The Mesopotamians used this dark, sticky

alluvial (uh-LOO-vee-uhl) gently sloping and formed from flood sediments

substance to waterproof boats and as mortar for the mud bricks they used to build their structures.

Although the Mesopotamians didn't know it, bitumen is an oil product, the first one ever used by humans. It was known by several names in Mesopotamia: the Sumerians called it *esir*, and the Akkadians knew it as *iddu*. The land was filled with bitumen deposits, black springs where the oil seeped out of the ground, and even bituminous rocks that released oil when heated. The best bitumen, though, was found on the south bank of the Euphrates River near the ancient cities of Hit and Ramadi. It was already softened by the water and ready to be used.

Bitumen hardens when it is dry.

The Ubaid culture was the first to realize that bitumen was useful for waterproofing. Their early boats were made from woven reeds covered with animal hides. When they discovered bitumen, they began using it to coat their boats on the inside and out, sealing the boat against moisture and strengthening the reed frames in the process. This technique remained unchanged throughout Mesopotamian history. The ancient Greek historian Herodotus visited Babylon and wrote, with some astonishment, that he saw "curious small round boats woven together of reeds, like baskets, and waterproofed with a coating of bitumen."

Some people still use bitumen as a sealant when building boats.

Bitumen's greatest use was as a building material. The Sumerians figured out that when mud was mixed with bitumen and then hardened in a kiln, it resulted in bricks that were hard as stone. The bricks were also waterproof. By the time of Nebuchadnezzar, bitumen was used to pave streets, waterproof bathhouses, and seal sewer pipes.

TRADING RESOURCES

Mesopotamia was rich in agriculture and livestock, so the Mesopotamians traded their surplus to foreign civilizations in exchange for other useful resources, such as metals and timber. Mesopotamian merchants loaded caravans and boats and traveled up and down the Persian Gulf, bringing timber from the Zagros Mountains, copper and tin from Anatolia, and gold from Egypt and the Indus Valley in India. Mesopotamian merchants and traders were so important in the ancient world that the Akkadian language and cuneiform script became the standard for communication and business throughout many civilizations.

The Zagros Mountains provided the Mesopotamians with valuable resources.

CHAPTER FOUR

MESOPOTAMIAN LIFE

Dadi, a priest in Ashur, once wrote the king of Assyria to explain that several of the royal shepherds had turned criminal:

Arbailayu and Girittu, the shepherds responsible for the [ritual] meals . . . refuse to come in for the tax collection. They do not fear the king. They rove about like runaways. I have now written them as follows: "Why do you not fear the king?" Ten men run around with them, draped with weapons, saying, "Whoever comes against us, we will cut down with bows."

The ancient Mesopotamians wrote letters by etching characters into wet clay.

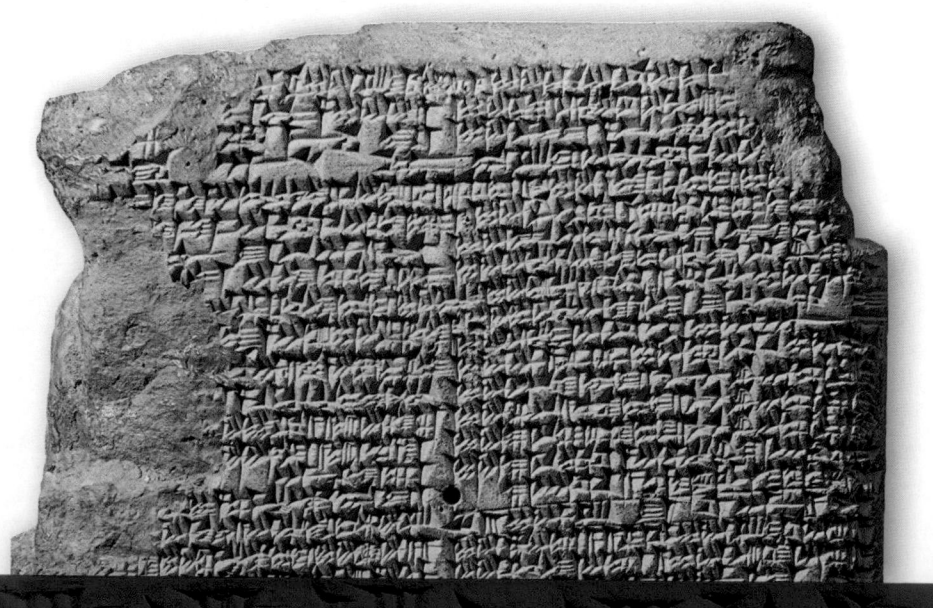

In addition to letters, the Mesopotamians used clay tablets for astronomical predictions and other documents.

There is no record of how the king responded to these rogue shepherds or whether they were ever caught and punished. Dadi wrote several other letters to the king to inform him about problems with deliveries, sacrifices, and other everyday issues. Dadi's letters, written on clay tablets, are only a few of the thousands of documents that have survived from ancient Mesopotamia. From legal contracts to lively descriptions of festivals, building projects, and even royal bathroom construction, these documents all provide intriguing glimpses into the lives of Mesopotamians who lived more than three thousand years ago.

A DAY AT SCHOOL

In about 2000 BCE, a Mesopotamian student recounted his normal school day: *I recited my tablet, ate my lunch, prepared my (new) tablet, wrote it, finished it; then my model tablets were brought to me; and in the afternoon my exercise tablets were brought to me. When school was dismissed, I went home, entered the house, and found my father sitting there. I explained my exercise-tablets to my father, recited my tablet to him, and he was delighted [. . .] When I arose early in the morning, I faced my mother and said to her, "Give me my lunch. I want to go to school!" My mother gave me two rolls, and I set out. In school the fellow in charge of punctuality said, "Why are you late?" Afraid and with pounding heart, I entered before my teacher and made a respectful curtsy.*

The experiences of this Mesopotamian student are not all that different from those of students today. Just like students today, he had to get to school on time and make sure his homework was done. Some things never change!

WHO THEY WERE, HOW THEY LIVED

According to the Code of Hammurabi, the wealthiest people in Mesopotamian society were called *awilum*. This group consisted of priests, government officials, professional soldiers, landowners, and merchants. The middle class, or *mushkenum*, was made up of free citizens who worked as merchants, farmers, artisans, and laborers. Slaves, who were called *wardum*, made up the lowest class.

The Mesopotamians believed that a person could move up or down in social class if the gods willed it. A wealthy merchant who had a lot of debt could lose his business and become a slave, or

Awilum made up the wealthiest class of Mesopotamian society.

a slave who was granted freedom could buy land and become an awilum. A person could also move up in society if he or she married someone in the higher class. Their children would automatically be a part of the higher class. This encouraged people to work hard to better themselves and the kingdom.

Slaves were either prisoners of war captured in battle or ordinary Mesopotamians who, for one reason or another, had fallen into bad luck. A person could become a slave if he or she assaulted

Wardum worked to serve the wishes of the higher classes.

someone. Mesopotamians could also volunteer themselves or their family members into slavery in order to pay off debts. Once a slave's term of service was finished, he or she could work jobs to earn money. Some slaves made enough money to buy their freedom.

Slaves were captured during wars or conquests of new territory.

Mesopotamian parents worked together to raise their children.

dowry (DOU-ree) money or property that a woman's family supplies to a man or his family in some cultures when the woman marries him

A MESOPOTAMIAN FAMILY

An average Mesopotamian family consisted of a mother, a father, and children. Mesopotamians called a family a "house," and all men were expected to "build a house," or have a family. Sometimes relatives such as parents, unmarried sisters, or younger brothers lived together. Girls became eligible for marriage when they were between fourteen and twenty years old, but boys did not generally marry until they were in their mid-twenties. The fathers of the bride and groom negotiated marriage arrangements. They agreed on a **dowry** that the bride would bring to the new marriage

66

and a bride price that the groom would pay. If the bride was too young to live with her new husband, she stayed in her father's house or with her new in-laws until she was older. Most marriages were **monogamous**, but there were rare cases when the husband could take a second wife, such as if his first wife became very sick or if she was unable to have children.

A woman's main job was to stay home and have children, but unmarried women, widows, and royal princesses often worked other jobs, such as being tavern keepers and priestesses. Women could conduct business and travel wherever they liked, but they first had to get permission from their husbands or fathers.

monogamous
(muh-NAH-guh-muss)
married to one person at a time

Prior to a marriage, the fathers of the bride and groom signed contracts promising to pay each other a certain fee.

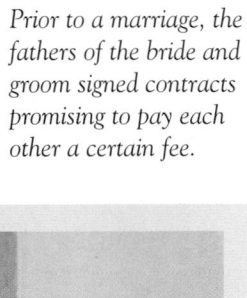

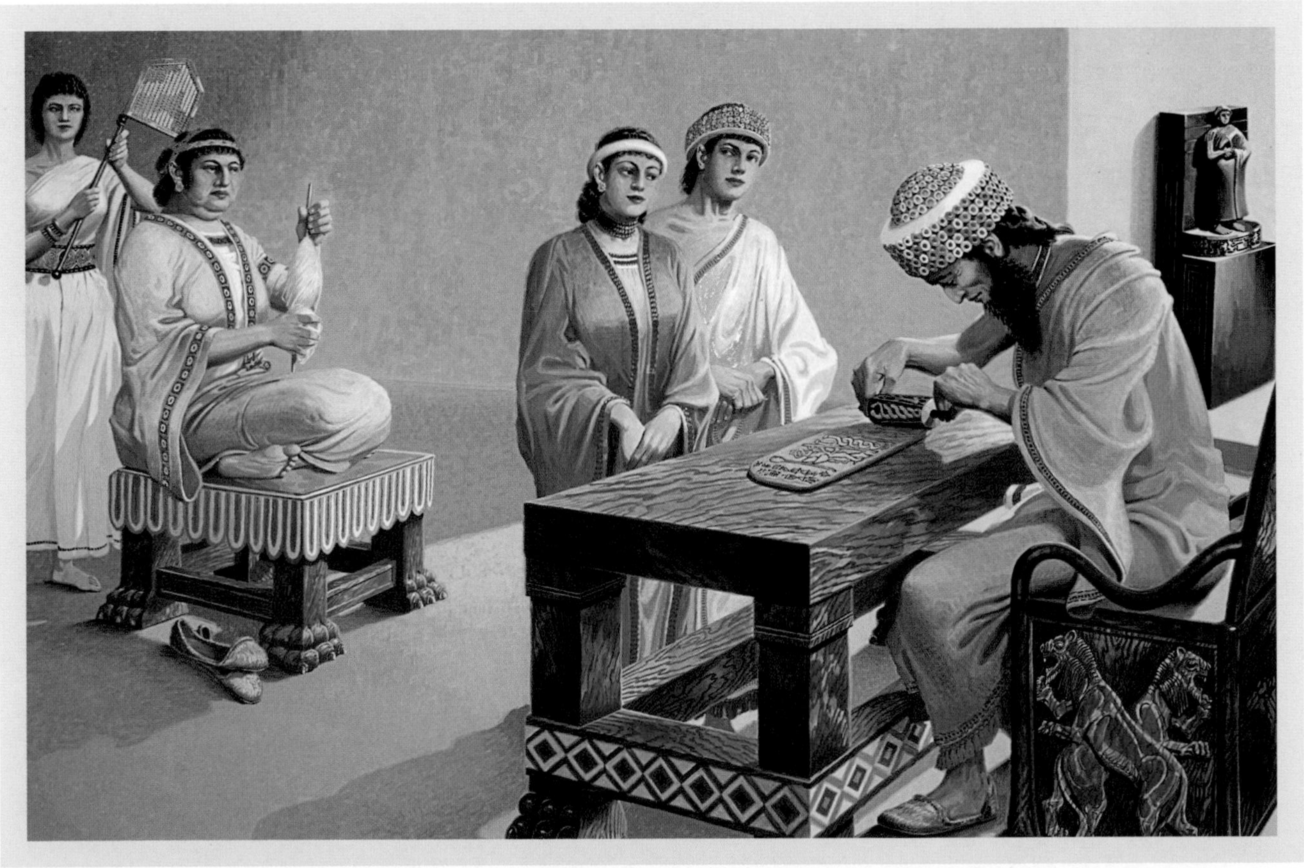

Mesopotamians, like people today, fell in love and hoped for happy marriages. Many clay tablets show loving couples with their arms entwined, often with children. Also like people today, Mesopotamians got depressed if someone they loved rejected them. When that happened, they recited charms or spells to the gods in hopes that they would bring the loved one back. One magic charm claimed that if a man used it, "this woman will speak to you the next time you see her and will be powerless to resist your charms."

Some families had many children.

HOME AND HEARTH

Urban families lived in one-story houses built of mud bricks, which were made from a mixture of clay and chopped straw and left to dry in the sun. Ordinary mud bricks weren't very strong, and houses often collapsed. Several laws in the Code of Hammurabi addressed this problem. One rule stated that a builder would be put to death if he made a house that fell and killed someone. Considering how many Mesopotamian city ruins exist today, it seems that the builders took that law very seriously. Bricks baked in a kiln lasted longer than sunbaked bricks, but were expensive to make. They were used only in royal structures, temples, and other important government buildings.

The size of a house depended on the wealth and status of its owners. Most people lived in small, windowless houses along narrow, winding streets and alleyways. Some houses had a second floor that was used as an open-air terrace, extra sleeping space, or storage. Rich Mesopotamians lived in spacious homes with many rooms surrounding an open courtyard. They had bedrooms,

Most Mesopotamians lived in very simple homes.

servants' quarters, and sometimes a private temple or chapel where they could worship their gods. Some homes even had indoor bathrooms consisting of a seat mounted above a pit or drain in the floor. A clay jar nearby held water that people used to flush waste through the drain and into the pipes below.

Mesopotamians did not use much furniture. Most houses usually contained a few stools, a table, and reed mats for beds and floor coverings. Wealthier people could afford wooden chairs or carved couches and wooden beds with mattresses, sheets, and blankets. Everyone stored their belongings in wooden chests, large clay jars, and baskets.

Wives or slaves cooked the family meals in an oven that was located either inside the house or in the courtyard outside. They used a surprising variety of tools to cook, including copper pots and pans, frying pans, hand mills to grind wheat and barley, mortars and pestles, and kettles. Utensils such as spoons, knives, and single-pronged forks were made of bronze, bone, or wood. Pots had small handles with holes for ropes so they could be hung out of the reach of mice and rats.

Mesopotamians ate very well. Even poorer people enjoyed rich spiced foods. They ate beef, lamb, pork, deer, fowl, and fish. Cheeses, breads, grains, vegetables, and fruits such as dates, apples, pears, figs, and pomegranates were common on every table. People cooked using milk, butter, animal fat, and sesame and olive oils. Everyone drank beer, which was much different from the beverage that people drink today. Mesopotamian beer was much weaker and often flavored with fruit or honey.

The Mesopotamians hunted a variety of animals for food and sport.

GOING TO SCHOOL

Most children, both boys and girls, were educated at home. The children of wealthy Mesopotamians often attended scribal school, to train as official scribes. Scribes held an important and respected position in society, and they often worked in the royal palaces or as high government officials.

These scribal schools, called "tablet houses," were attended mainly by boys, though there were some female students. Teachers were known as "fathers of the tablet-house." Students started school around age five and spent their days memorizing and writing cuneiform words, reading aloud, and copying texts to practice their writing

Scribes occupied a respected position in Mesopotamian society.

skills. Many school tablets have been unearthed. They display a
teacher's writing on one side and a student's work on the other.

    Reading and writing were not the only skills taught in scribal
school. Students also had to learn grammar, spelling, mathematics,
different types of handwriting, and how to make a clay envelope
and seal a document. Once a student mastered all of this, he or she
could leave the school to become a professional scribe.

*Becoming a scribe
required years of study.*

CITY LIFE, COUNTRY LIFE

The larger Mesopotamian cities were enormous urban centers. Some were home to tens of thousands of people. Most cities were divided into three sections. An inner walled section held the palace, the temples, and homes for nobility and wealthy citizens. The outer city held houses, farms, fields, and gardens. The wharf area was home to merchants and tavern keepers. It was also where ships docked and unloaded their trade goods. Artists and craftspeople, such as bead makers, potters, weavers, and weapon makers, had shops around the city. Administrative areas called wards held offices and homes of city elders and government officials.

Elaborately decorated temples were the center of city activity. Most city dwellers worked for either the temples or the palace in some way. These places employed priests, builders, scribes, cooks, bakers, musicians, slaves, and administrative officers.

Merchants and artisans sold their goods in the wharf areas of ancient Mesopotamian cities.

Musicians were often hired to play in the king's court.

Mesopotamian musicians played a variety of string, wind, and percussion instruments.

Cities were generally dirty places where people threw their garbage out into the street to be dried in the sun and walked on. Pigs, dogs, and rats roamed the streets and scavenged the rubbish for food. Many cities and towns had drainage systems of clay pipes that removed rainwater and some garbage from the streets. The waste flowed out of the city and into the nearby river.

Country life was focused on producing food and livestock for the cities. Many farmers were ordered by the king or the priests to provide temples with food and sacrifices. The lands outlying the cities were dotted with smaller villages that had their own mayors

Nomads often used the resources of towns and cities, but did not make permanent homes there.

and councils of elders. Mesopotamian law stated that these villages were responsible for any crimes that happened within their boundaries. The city council had the power to sell or redistribute land and ration water rights. Many nomadic tribes wandered the countryside, usually herding animals such as sheep and goats. They stayed near water sources and used villages and cities as home bases.

WHAT TO WEAR

Mesopotamians loved to dress well, no matter where or when they lived. Before people learned how to weave fabric from sheep's wool, they wore leather and animal skins. Women secured their clothing with large pins that were hung with strings of beads. After the weaving loom was invented, people wore rich textiles made of wool, linen, and silk. These garments were dyed in beautiful colors and decorated with beads and embroidery. A man's wardrobe included soft tunics and lengths of fabric that were draped over one shoulder. Women also wore long fabrics that were draped and pinned over their shoulders. Men and women alike wore jewelry such as earrings and bracelets. Women piled their long hair into elaborate styles and secured it with hairpins made of bone, copper, silver, or gold. Men usually wore their hair very short and grew long wavy beards.

Mesopotamian men did not always wear shirts.

CHAPTER FIVE

BEAUTY, FAITH, AND ART

From 1922 to 1934, a British archaeologist named Leonard Woolley excavated the ruins of the ancient city of Ur. His most amazing find was a cemetery with more than eighteen

The artifacts found at the Ur excavation changed the way modern scholars thought about Mesopotamian art.

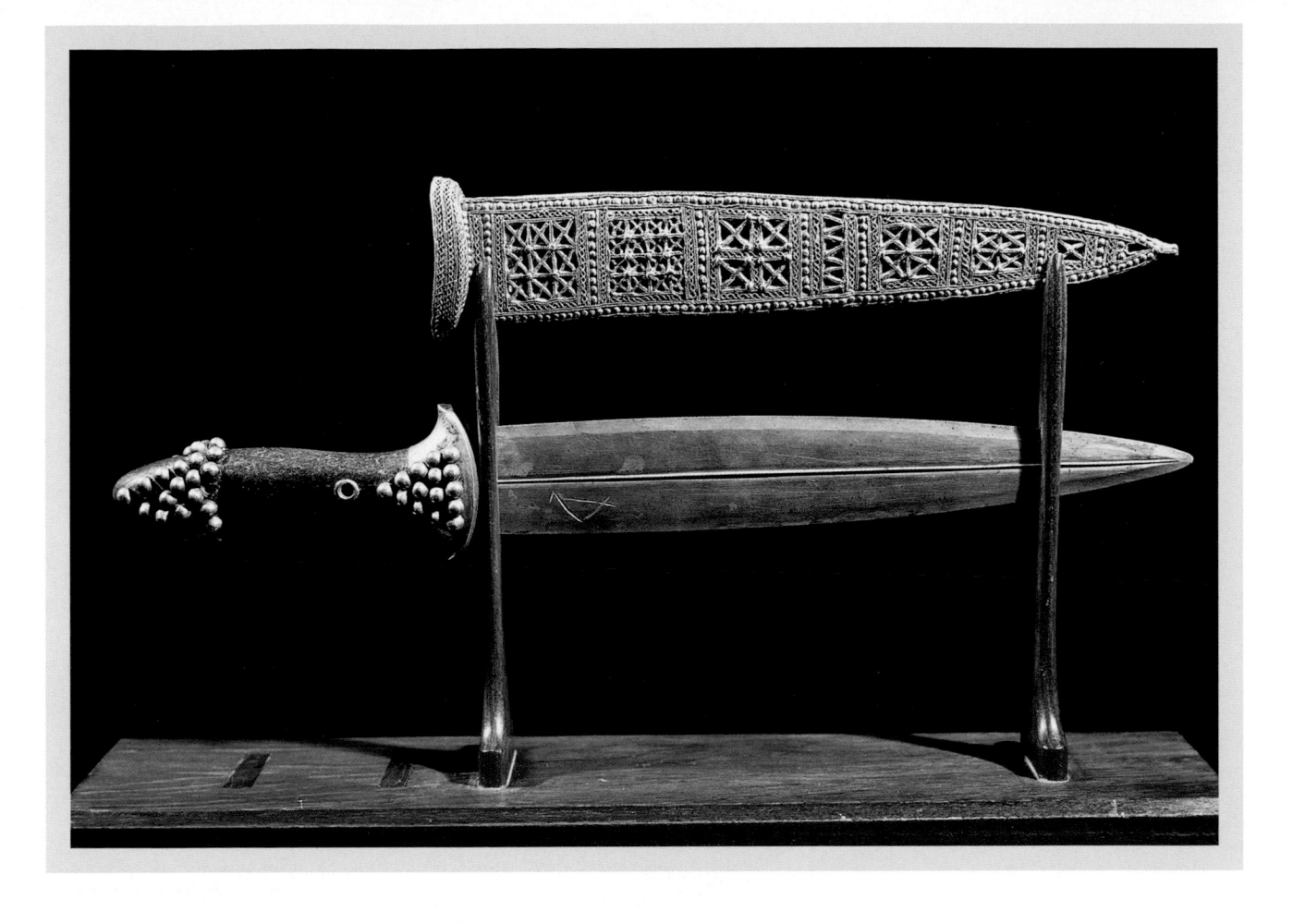

hundred graves. The graves were filled with golden objects and other riches. Until then, no one had imagined that the ancient Mesopotamians had such beauty and art in their culture.

Mesopotamians filled their lives with beautiful art, music, and stories. But they didn't usually create art for art's sake. Most of their art was made to honor and worship the gods and goddesses or to celebrate victories in battle. Rulers used artwork to express their power throughout the cities, temples, and palaces of Mesopotamia. The more artwork that decorated these spaces, the more powerful the kings and gods appeared to be.

Even practical objects such as knives had artistic qualities.

The Past Is Present
RIGHT ON TIME

Have you ever wondered why an hour is made up of 60 minutes, or why there are 60 seconds in each minute? The Babylonians were especially interested in the number 60. They based many numerical calculations on a "base 60 form." The way we tell time today is because of the Babylonians. We also measure a circle as 360 degrees, another Babylonian base 60 invention.

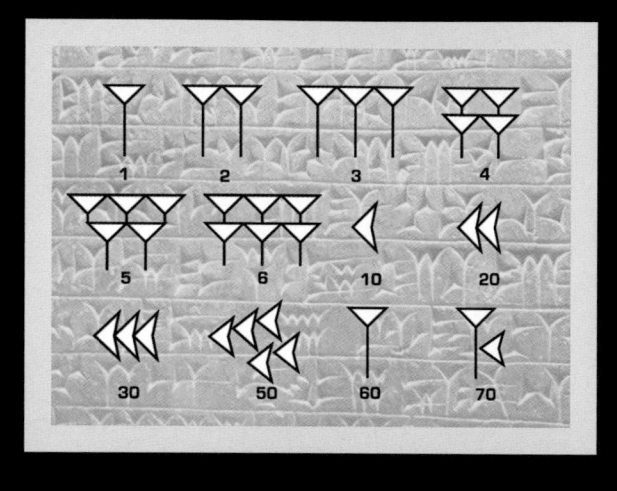

The Babylonians are also partially responsible for the 24-hour day. A Babylonian day began at sunset and consisted of 12 hours, each hour twice as long as the ones we measure today. Greek astronomers later took the Babylonian idea and separated the 12 double hours into 24 hours, creating the 24-hour day that the world uses today.

Most statues were images of gods and goddesses. They were used in temples and rituals to represent the gods themselves. The largest and most ornate statues were reserved for palaces and temples. Ordinary people often had smaller statues at home for personal worship.

GODS, GODDESSES, DEMONS, AND MONSTERS

The Mesopotamian people were **polytheistic**, and they believed that their **deities** controlled every aspect of their lives. Each city

polytheistic (pol-ee-thee-ISS-tik) believing in more than one god

deities (DEE-i-teez) gods or goddesses

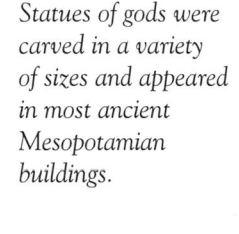

Statues of gods were carved in a variety of sizes and appeared in most ancient Mesopotamian buildings.

and each kingdom was protected by a certain deity known as a patron god or patron goddess. It was the duty of the city's ruler to act on the patron god's behalf. The king was responsible for maintaining the temples, overseeing rituals, and holding festivals to receive the gods' blessings.

In most Mesopotamian cities, large towerlike temples rose high in the air at the center of town. These structures, known as ziggurats, were built from steplike platforms. Their outside walls

Ziggurats were among the ancient Mesopotamians' most impressive construction projects.

were covered with dazzling, colorful glazed bricks that depicted animals and scenes from the lives of the gods. People climbed ramps to reach shrines perched at the tops of the ziggurats.

The patron god or goddess of the city had the biggest temple, but other shrines and smaller temples to lesser deities stood nearby. As a city grew in stature and power, its patron god also became more important. The god Marduk, for instance, was the patron god of Babylon and became a major god when Babylon was the capital city.

Mesopotamians believed that a god literally lived in its temple. As a result, they built temples to be as comfortable as possible. The god or goddess rested in the temple's innermost room, where the statue of the deity stood. Every day, the temple priests washed, clothed, and perfumed the statue. Plates of breads and foods were set before the statue as the sounds of music, hymns, and prayers filled the air. On festival days and other religious holidays, the statues were taken from their temples and carried through the streets amid singing and dancing.

Marduk was one of the most prominent gods of ancient Mesopotamian religion.

Nanna (right) was the god of the moon.

The Mesopotamians worshipped deities of health, luck, wealth, home, childbirth, and many other parts of daily life. Most people worshipped a personal deity or god, and they felt as if their personal luck and fortune were attached to the god. Daily prayers were said and sacrifices were made to keep the god happy.

Sometimes the gods sent messages down to earth in the form of signs and omens. Special priests used **divination** to interpret the gods' messages. The Mesopotamians considered divination to be a scientific method of understanding these messages, and priests spent years learning the different signs and omens that the

divination (di-vuh-NAY-shuhn) the practice of foretelling the future by interpreting signs in nature

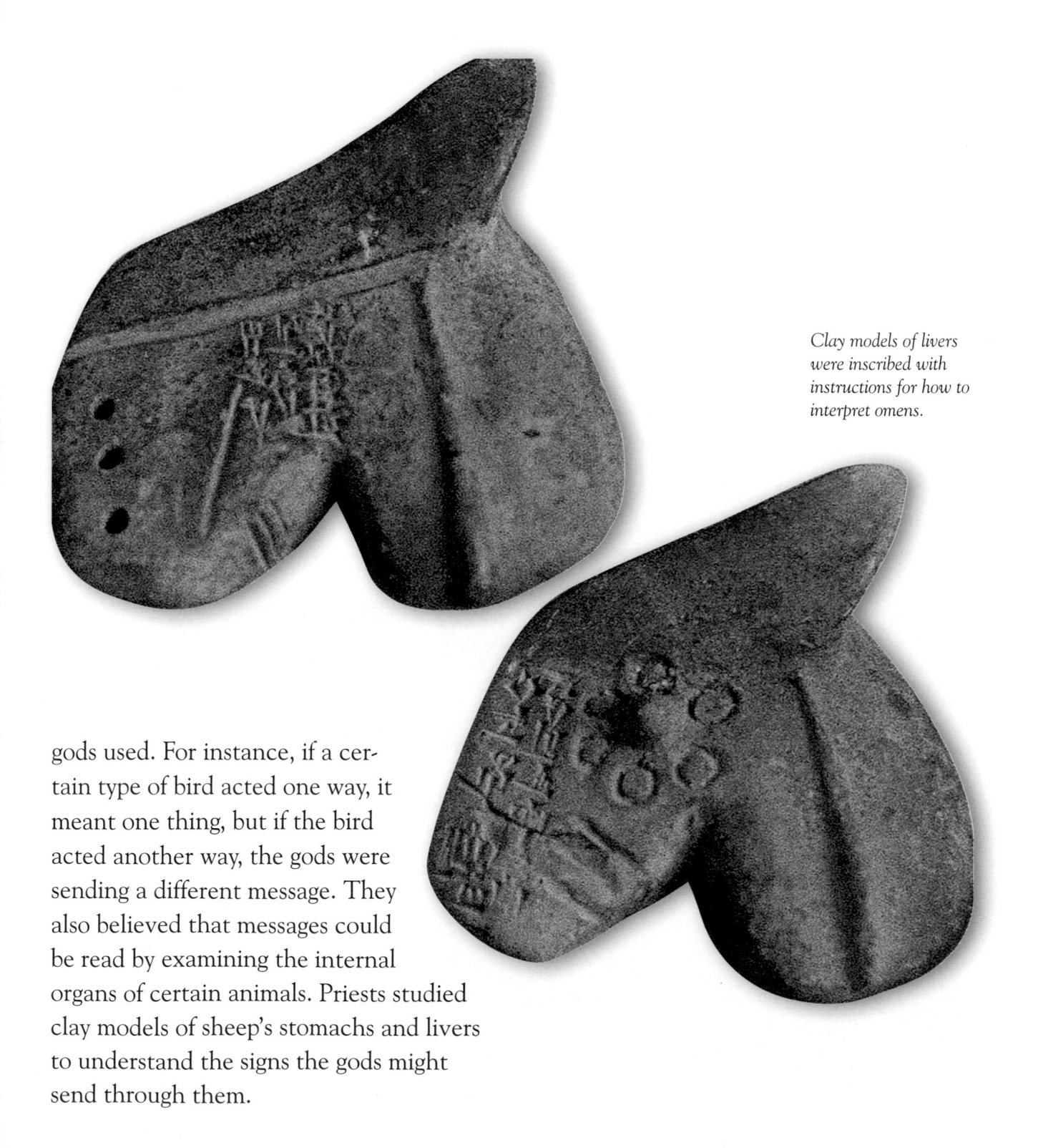

Clay models of livers were inscribed with instructions for how to interpret omens.

gods used. For instance, if a certain type of bird acted one way, it meant one thing, but if the bird acted another way, the gods were sending a different message. They also believed that messages could be read by examining the internal organs of certain animals. Priests studied clay models of sheep's stomachs and livers to understand the signs the gods might send through them.

READING AND WRITING

Early in Mesopotamian history, people needed a way to keep records of food, animals, crops, and other items. At first, they used crude counting devices such as sticks and small clay tokens. As the city-states grew, though, this method became too cumbersome. The Sumerians began to write on soft clay tablets.

The earliest forms of writing were pictographs, or drawings that represented actual things. The oldest tablets date to about 3100 BCE. Over the centuries, the pictographs grew simpler until they became a series of marks in the clay. This method of writing, called cuneiform, was the world's first written language.

The Mesopotamians used reeds with a triangular point to etch cuneiform writing into clay.

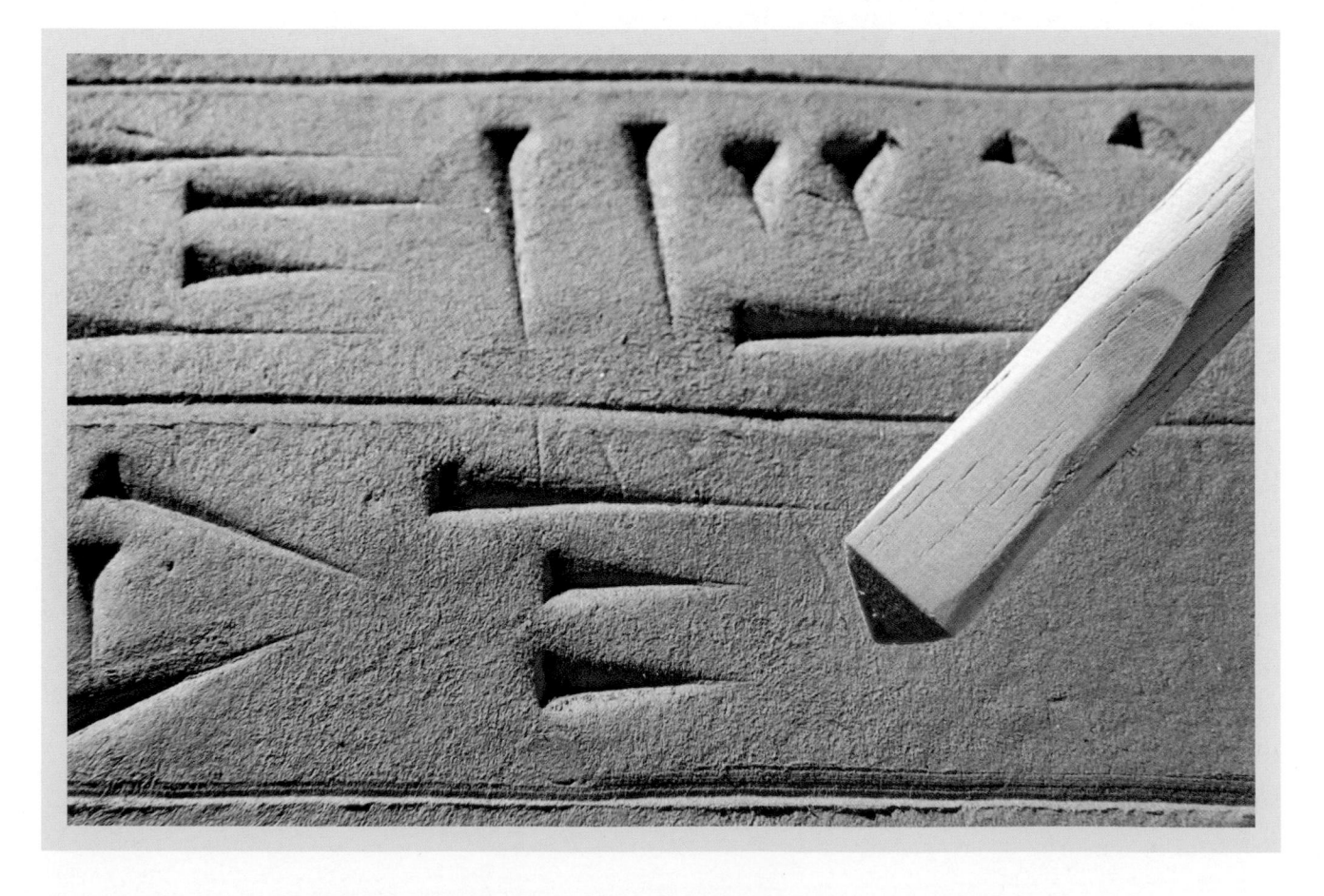

Most cuneiform tablets were written with a reed stylus. When the scribe pressed the stylus into the wet clay, it left a mark. When the clay dried, the writing became permanent. Scribes also wrote on wax tablets by etching the words into the soft wax. The scribe could erase the writing by rubbing the wax smooth again. Cuneiform eventually spread throughout Mesopotamia and to other areas, and continued to be used until about 75 CE. Gradually, though, people forgot how to read it.

When rolled onto soft clay, cylinders created impressions of the images and words inscribed on their surface.

contagious (kuhn-TAY-juhs) spread by direct or indirect contact with an infected person or animal

That changed in 1835, when inscriptions were found on a cliff at Behistun in modern-day Iran. The inscriptions, carved during the reign of King Darius of Persia (reigned 522–486 BCE), included identical texts in three different languages: Old Persian, Babylonian, and a language called Elamite. Experts translated the Persian, then set to work on the other symbols. They eventually cracked the code by comparing the unfamiliar languages to the Persian words that they already knew. This work allowed scholars to decipher ancient Sumerian, Assyrian, and Babylonian clay tablets for the first time in more than a thousand years.

Sometime around 5000 BCE, someone, perhaps a scribe, got an idea. He carved a scene into a small cylinder. When the cylinder was rolled onto wet clay, the scene made an impression in the clay. The first Mesopotamian clay cylinder was created. These seals were used frequently throughout Mesopotamia, mainly to stamp official or administrative documents. The seals sometimes showed scenes from religious stories or triumphant battles.

MESOPOTAMIAN MEDICINE

Ancient Mesopotamians believed that sickness and injury were some-times punishments handed down from the gods. However, they also realized that people had the power to cure a variety of illnesses. They knew that some illnesses were the result of hot or cold temperatures, overeating, consuming spoiled food, or drinking too much alcohol. They even understood that some diseases were **contagious**.

Two types of doctors practiced in ancient Mesopotamia. The *asipu* used magical cures, while the *asu*

These cylinders use pictures to tell part of the Mesopotamian legend of Gilgamesh.

The asipu used cures based on religion and folklore rather than on science.

was more like a modern medical doctor. Kings, nobles, and other wealthy people could afford to visit both kinds of doctors when they were sick or hurt.

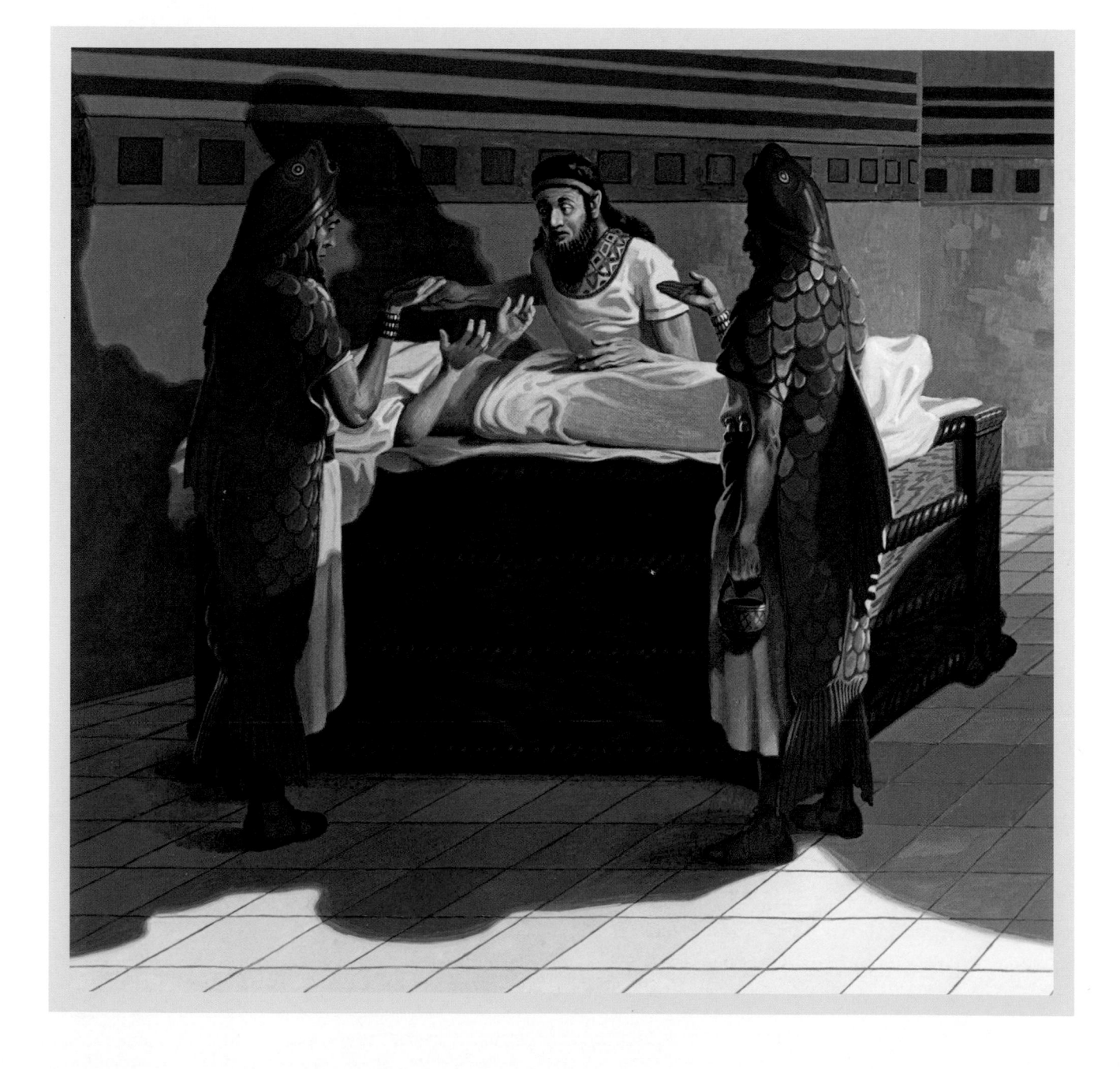

ASTRONOMY

The Babylonians were famous for their knowledge of astronomy and the heavens. They discovered that they could measure time by watching the sky, so they began keeping detailed records of the movements and positions of stars, the moon, planets, and other heavenly bodies. This helped them decide the best times to plant crops. It also helped them plan religious festivals. One of the greatest innovations to come from the Babylonian's study of astronomy was the development of an accurate calendar.

The earliest Babylonian calendars were lunar, which means they were based on the moon's cycle. Each lunar month was 29 or 30 days long. A year was approximately 354 days. The calendar would go off track every few years, so the Babylonians added an extra month every three years to realign it. In about the 4th century BCE, the Babylonians realized that the dates of the phases of the moon repeated exactly after 19 years. They created a new, more accurate calendar based on this system, which became the basis for the calendar we use today.

MATHEMATICS

Mesopotamians had one of the earliest written numbering systems, which remained in use throughout the course of their civilization. Numbers are found on the oldest known clay tablet, which dates back to about 3100 BCE, as well as on the most recent text discovered, which dates to 75 BCE. The Mesopotamians were the first to invent the "place value" system of counting. This means that a digit in a number has a different value based on where it is in the number. For example, the digit "3" means three in the number 63. It means 30 in the number 432, and 300 in the number 1,398.

CHAPTER SIX

THE LEGACY OF MESOPOTAMIA

Cyrus of Persia's invasion of Babylon in 539 BCE signaled the end of the Mesopotamian civilization. Babylon and much of the rest of Mesopotamia were absorbed into the

Cyrus was a fair ruler who improved life for many Babylonians.

Around the time of Cyrus's conquest, Babylon had begun to fall from its former glory.

Persian Empire. But things had already been in decline for the Mesopotamians for some time before that. Their cities had become overcrowded, and it was getting harder to feed everyone. The climate was changing, too. The rivers began changing course, taking water away from the cities.

Under Cyrus's leadership, change came very slowly. After he conquered Babylon, Cyrus allowed the city's people to continue living there and practicing their own faiths. He treated the Mesopotamians with respect, even declaring new laws that made life better for everyone. But eventually, people left or were forced out of the old Mesopotamian cities, which fell into ruin and were forgotten.

The people and civilizations of ancient Mesopotamia left behind a rich legacy of inventions and ideas that became the building blocks of many civilizations that developed in later years. The

Ancient Egyptian writing systems may have been influenced by the Mesopotamians.

most important lasting legacy of Mesopotamia is the invention of writing. Sumerian was possibly the first written language in the ancient world. The writing system began with crude pictographs of objects. It eventually evolved into a complex type of handwriting. Mesopotamian cuneiform writing may have also influenced many other languages, including ancient Egyptian hieroglyphs, Indus Valley writing, and Chinese characters.

The Mesopotamians figured out how to plow, plant, nurture, and harvest crops. They constructed the first known agricultural tools, including plows and hoes. Their irrigation systems enabled them to grow more food, which eventually led to the development of city-states.

The Mesopotamians delighted in the world around them and strove to understand how it worked. They made lists of plants, animals, minerals, and other aspects of the natural world. They studied the stars and created the first astronomical calculations, calendars, and measurements. They were the first to try to heal the sick and injured by studying symptoms and giving medicines. They even created mathematical systems that are still in use today.

From the earliest nomads who were the first to grow their own food to the wealthy and powerful Babylonian civilization, many of the basic elements of world culture today are based on the traditions begun by the cultures of Mesopotamia.

WRITING IT DOWN

The ancient Mesopotamians made many lasting contributions to society, and some of their greatest achievements have to do with the written word. The Sumerians were among the first civilizations to create literature, writing down epic tales of gods and battles. One of the most famous stories, *The Epic of Gilgamesh*, is still read today. It consists of twelve incomplete tablets of poetry, and it details the adventures of Gilgamesh, the legendary king of Uruk.

The Mesopotamians also recorded everyday life events such as marriages, deaths, sales, and legal agreements, just as we do today. They were the first people to write and send letters. They also wrote myths, prayers, and hymns, many of which influenced other writings of the ancient world.

BIOGRAPHIES

ASHURBANIPAL (REIGNED 668–627 BCE) was the last great king of Assyria. In 648 BCE, he attacked Babylon and killed many of its citizens. Under Ashurbanipal, Assyria became a powerful kingdom in Mesopotamia. The Assyrian Empire collapsed and disappeared a few years after his death.

CYRUS THE GREAT (REIGNED 559–529 BCE) is considered to be the founder of the Persian Empire. He captured Babylon in 539 BCE. Cyrus was the son of nobility and an excellent military commander. He was admired as a liberator rather than a conqueror because he respected the customs of other cultures in his kingdom.

GILGAMESH (REIGNED CA. 2700 BCE) was a semilegendary king of Mesopotamia who later became the hero in an epic story. He was credited with building the walls of Uruk.

HAMMURABI (REIGNED CA. 1792–1750 BCE) united Babylonia into one nation with the capital at Babylon. His rule began the Old Babylonian period.

Herodotus (5th century BCE) was a Greek historian and traveler. He is known as the father of history because he was one of the first to write the histories of other cultures. His book, *History,* includes many descriptions of Mesopotamia and Babylon.

Nebuchadnezzar II (reigned 605–ca. 561 BCE) was a great military leader who became king of Babylonia in 605 BCE. During his reign, he rebuilt Babylon into a great city.

Sargon the Great (reigned ca. 2334–2279 BCE) conquered Mesopotamia and established the Akkadian empire.

Leonard Woolley (1880–1960 CE) was a British archaeologist who made many of the first important discoveries in Mesopotamia. He is best known for excavating the Royal Cemetery at Ur and is considered one of the first modern archaeologists.

TIMELINE

7000–4000 BCE: *The Hassuna, Samarra, and Halaf cultures grow. Sumer emerges in southern Mesopotamia.*

| 10,000 BCE | 7000 BCE | 4000 BCE |

6200–4000 BCE: *The Ubaid culture builds the earliest Mesopotamian temples and structures. Early irrigation systems transform agriculture.*

10,000 BCE: *The first humans migrate to Mesopotamia and begin to develop cities and agriculture in the region.*

3100 BCE: *Pictographic writing is invented. The first known mathematical tables and problems are recorded.*

CA. 2700 BCE: *The legendary Gilgamesh rules Uruk.*

2600 BCE: *The first royals are buried in the Royal Cemetery at Ur.*

2400 BCE: *Pictograph writing develops into cuneiform writing.*

3OOO BCE

2OOO BCE

2100 BCE: *The Sumerian King List is written.*

2350 BCE: *Sargon the Great unifies Sumer and Akkad into one Mesopotamian kingdom.*

1792–1750 BCE:
Hammurabi conquers Babylon and begins his empire.

1595 BCE: *The Hittites conquer Babylon and control Mesopotamia.*

1234 BCE: *Tukulti-Ninurta of Assyria attacks Babylon and becomes king of the Assyrian empire.*

1500 BCE   **1000 BCE**

704 BCE: *Nineveh becomes the capital of Assyria.*

704–681 BCE: *Mesopotamia is ruled by the Assyrian king Sennacherib.*

669–627 BCE: *Ashurbanipal, the last great Assyrian king, rules Mesopotamia.*

612 BCE: *Nabopolassar captures the Assyrian city of Nineveh.*

612–539 BCE: *The Neo-Babylonian period*

605–561 BCE: *King Nebuchadnezzar II rebuilds Babylon.*

500 BCE   O

75 BCE: *Alexander the Great conquers the Persians.*

331 BCE: *The last known cuneiform text is written.*

539 BCE: *Cyrus the Great of Persia conquers Babylon, leading to the end of the Mesopotamian Empire.*

CA. 561 BCE: *King Nebuchadnezzar II dies.*

GLOSSARY

agriculture (AG-ri-kuhl-chur) the raising of crops and animals

alluvial (uh-LOO-vee-uhl) gently sloping and formed from flood sediments

ambassadors (am-BAS-uh-dorz) officials sent by a government to represent it in another country

archaeologists (ahr-kee-AH-luh-jists) people who study the past, which often involves digging up old buildings, objects, and bones and examining them carefully

contagious (kuhn-TAY-juhs) spread by direct or indirect contact with an infected person or animal

deities (DEE-i-teez) gods or goddesses

divination (di-vuh-NAY-shuhn) the practice of foretelling the future by interpreting signs in nature

domesticate (duh-MES-ti-kate) to tame plants or animals so they can be used by humans

dowry (DOU-ree) money or property that a woman's family supplies to a man or his family in some cultures when the woman marries him

empire (EM-pire) a group of countries or states that have the same ruler

fertile (FUR-tuhl) good for growing crops and plants

flax (FLAKS) a plant with blue flowers that produces oil and fiber

hereditary (huh-RED-i-ter-ee) passed down from parent to child

irrigation (ir-uh-GAY-shuhn) the use of artificial means, such as channels and pipes, to supply water to crops

monogamous (muh-NAH-guh-muss) married to one person at a time

nomads (NO-madz) members of a community who travel from place to place instead of living in the same place all the time

omens (OH-muhnz) signs or warnings about the future

plundered (PLUHN-durd) stole things by force

polytheistic (pol-ee-thee-ISS-tik) believing in more than one god

FIND OUT MORE

BOOKS

Apte, Sunita. *Mesopotamia*. New York: Children's Press, 2010.

Schomp, Virginia. *Ancient Mesopotamia: The Sumerians, Babylonians, and Assyrians*. New York: Children's Press, 2005.

Shuter, Jane. *Mesopotamia*. Chicago: Heinemann-Raintree, 2005.

Steele, Philip, and John Farndon. DK Eyewitness Books: *Mesopotamia*. New York: DK Publishing, 2007.

Visit this Scholastic Web site for more information on Ancient Mesopotamia:
www.factsfornow.scholastic.com
Enter the keywords **Ancient Mesopotamia**

INDEX

Page numbers in *italics* indicate a photograph or map.

ABOUT THE AUTHOR

Allison Lassieur has written more than eighty books about history, world cultures, ancient civilizations, science, and current events. She lives with her husband in Tennessee.